What people are saying about...

Accessible Apologetics and Mikel Del Rosario

Mikel Del Rosario is one of the brightest young apologists on the scene today. Not just because he really knows the best arguments so well, but because he can communicate them in such a stimulating way. *Accessible Apologetics* will help you raise the bar of learning in your church.

Dr. Craig Hazen
Founder and Director of the Master of Arts program in Christian Apologetics program at Biola University and author of *Five Sacred Crossings.*

I'm excited about Mikel Del Rosario's work on behalf of apologetics. I'm supporting his teaching, his speaking ministry and his training program.

Dr. J.P. Moreland
Distinguished Professor of Philosophy at Talbot School of Theology and author of *Kingdom Triangle* and *The God Question.*

Mikel is a clear, articulate communicator.
He is gifted with the ability to connect with his audience in a manner that is both accessible and memorable.

I recommend his apologetics ministry with confidence to those looking to be better equipped to understand and defend Christianity in today's secular culture.

Brian Auten
Founder of *Apologetics315* and director of Reasonable Faith Belfast.

ACCESSIBLE
APOLOGETICS
WORKBOOK

Apologetics Guy^{SM}

Five Lessons for Everyday Defenders of the Faith

Workbook Contents

Introduction to Lesson 1

"*But in your hearts set apart Christ as Lord. Always be prepared to give an answer to everyone who asks you to give the reason for the hope that you have. But do this with gentleness and respect.*"

- Peter, the Apostle (1 Peter 3:15 NIV)

> # Lesson 1: Outline
>
> **Introduction to Apologetics**
> I. What is Christian Apologetics?
> II. Why Defend the Faith?

Want to study Apologetics?

You won't be sorry!

An "apologetic" is simply a defense. Peter actually commanded all believers to be ready with answers when people ask us about our faith. In **1 Peter 3:15**, the word translated as "answer" is the word *apologia*, which means "a reasoned statement or argument."[1]

Obeying this command just means you've got reasons for what you believe and you're ready to talk with anyone who's got questions. It doesn't mean getting defensive. It doesn't mean getting into fights. It means speaking the truth in love as we represent our Lord at work, at school, in our community and society. But in order to be prepared, **we've got to know what we believe and why we believe it**.

---

[1] Thayer and Smith, "Apologia - Greek Lexion," StudyLight.org, http://www.studylight.org/lex/grk/view.cgi?number=627 (accessed June 4, 2010).

That's what this course in defending the faith is all about—increasing your confidence as a Christian by exploring the reasons and evidences for the faith, and preparing yourself to be a more effective ambassador of Jesus Christ.

Defend without being defensive

Even if you're totally new to this, there's apologetic value in a confident believer's simply remaining calm under fire. Many people who oppose the faith often repeat slogans they've heard but never really considered: "The Bible's full of contradictions," "Christians are intolerant," "All religions are basically the same."

Relax. **No need to get defensive.** <u>Remember that the truth is on our side, and lies are not defensible.</u>

One of my favorite radio show hosts, Greg Koukl, often says that apologetics can "look more like diplomacy than combat."[2] I like that.

Sincerely asking questions like "What do you mean by that?" or "How did you come to that conclusion?" can help critics consider what *they* believe and why *they* believe it—perhaps for the first time. And if you're stumped by a question, it's no problem to say, "Let me think about that and get back to you." Afterwards, do your homework and look it up. You'll find there are good answers to the hard questions.

---

[2] Koukl also mentions this in Ravi Zacharias et al., *To Everyone an Answer: A Case for the Christian Worldview: Essays in Honor of Norman L. Geisler*, ed. Francis J. Beckwith, William Lane Craig, James Porter Moreland and Norman L. Geisler (Downers Grove, Ill.: IVP Academic, 2004), 48.

ar·gue

(ahr-gue) verb

1. To present reasons for or against a thing.
2. To contend in oral disagreement.
3. To state the reasons for or against.

Dictionary.com Unabridged. Based on the *Random House Dictionary*, © Random House, Inc. 2010.

Argue without being argumentative

When we say "argue," we don't mean getting into fights. Paul said we shouldn't be mean, contentious or going around looking for a fight (2 Tim. 2:24). But he didn't say we couldn't have arguments in the sense of having reasoned disagreements about important issues.

In fact, he said we should humbly teach those who oppose the truth so they could "come to their senses" and be saved (2 Timothy 2:25-26). Because of this, **we're going to study some of the best arguments for the truth of the Christian faith together.**

Part of loving God with our minds (Mark 12:30) is using our mental faculties to draw conclusions about Him and His world based on Scripture, observation, and careful thinking. Indeed, the ability to argue well is important for rational discussion about spiritual matters. In this sense, <u>an argument is actually a good thing because it helps us discover and clearly communicate truth.</u>

Speak the truth in love

Are we ready to do the hard work of discovering truth and defending it against error? If not, we may fall prey to the latest piece of misinformation popularized by our culture through music, movies or literature. Consider the connection between truth, love and discipleship:

> "Then we will no longer be infants, tossed back and forth by the waves, and blown here and there by every wind of teaching and by the cunning and craftiness of men in their deceitful scheming. Instead, **speaking the truth in love**, we will in all things grow up into him who is the Head, that is, Christ."
>
> - **Paul, the Apostle** (Ephesians 4:14-15 NIV)

This literally means "*truthing* in love," and includes the ideas of "living" and "doing" the truth.[3] Here's the point: Since the church grows in maturity through truth and love, **false ideas and unloving attitudes are major obstacles to our discipleship.** If becoming like Jesus is our end goal, "speaking the truth in love" is an important part of getting there.

If we're doing this, gentleness and respect will be a natural part of our apologetic. Unfortunately, some Christians are quick to quote **1 Peter 3:15**, but don't really live out the command because they treat the last part of the verse like a suggestion. **It's not.** And it doesn't honor God when we act like jerks. We've got to study and present the truth—not for the sake of winning arguments or looking smart—but because we love God and love people. It's an obedience thing. It's a love thing. And when people come to faith, it's always a God thing.

Let's embark on this course together as an act of discipleship to Jesus.

---

[3] John R.W. Stott, *Message of Ephesians: God's New Society (The Bible Speaks Today)*, New Ed ed. (Downers Grove: Inter-Varsity Press, 1984), 172.

Lesson 1:

Why Defend My Faith?

a·pol·o·get·ics
(uh-pol-uh-jet-iks) noun

1. The branch of theology that is concerned with defending or proving the truth of Christian doctrines.
2. Formal argumentation in defense of something, such as a position or system.

The American Heritage® *Dictionary of the English Language*, Fourth Edition. Houghton Mifflin Company, 2004. Dictionary.com

I.   What is Christian Apologetics?

A. About the Discipline

1. It's a _____ discipline:

    "Apologetics is that branch of Christian theology which seeks
    to provide a rational justification for the truth claims of the
    Christian faith."

    — William Lane Craig[4]

2. It has _____ application:

3. There's _____ apologetics:

---

[4] William Lane Craig, *Reasonable Faith: Christian Truth and Apologetics*, 3 ed. (Wheaton:
Crossway Books, 2008), 15.

4. There's _____ apologetics:

"Apologetics is simply to defend the faith, and thereby
destroy arguments and every proud obstacle against the
knowledge of God (2 Cor. 10:5). It is opening the door,
clearing the rubble, and getting rid of the hurdles so that
people can come to Christ." –Norman Geisler[5]

5. It involves _____   _____:

[5] Quoted by Josh McDowell in *To Everyone an Answer,* 9.

B. Three Essential Elements of Apologetics

1. To understand the answers to tough questions about Christianity
2. To give good answers to those who ask tough questions about Christianity
3. To share those answers in a wise and tactical manner in our apologetic encounters

II.   Why Defend My Faith?[6]

A. _____ Gave People _____ to _____.

1. "Jesus demonstrated the truth of His message and his identity over and over again, using nearly every method at his disposal, including miracle, prophecy, godly style of life, authoritative teaching *and* reasoned argumentation."

   – Craig Hazen[7]

2. Acts 1:3

---

[6] Adapted from "Defending the Defense of the Faith" in *To Everyone an Answer*, 37-46.
[7] *Ibid.* 39.

B. Case Study: Healing of the Paralytic (Mark 2:1-12)

1. First, Jesus said, "Your sins are forgiven."

2. Then, he did a miracle and healed the man. Why?

3. Relevant scriptures:

    a. Isaiah 35:5-6

    b. Luke 11:29

    b. 1 Kings 18:20-45

    c. Isaiah 41:21-22

C. Jesus' Disciples Provided Reasons to Believe

1. Jesus' disciples followed His example and told other believers to do the same thing.

   a. _____ gave people reasons to believe.

   b. _____ told believers to contend for the faith (Jude 3)

   c. _____ believed eyewitness testimony and careful history would help Theophilus know with certainty that the things he was taught are true. That's why he wrote Luke-Acts (Luke 1:1-4).

   d. _____ said to always be ready to give a reason for the hope you have in Jesus, but with humility and respect (1 Peter 3:15).

   e. _____ was explaining and proving that Jesus was the Messiah. Because of this, many Jews and God-fearing Greeks in Thessalonica were *persuaded* and joined them (Acts 17:2-4)

2. The Holy Spirit has used believers who _____,

   _____, and present _____ to lead people to salvation in Christ.

Christian Objections to Studying Apologetics

- "People don't come to faith in Christ through apologetics."
- "Without faith, it's impossible to please God."
- "Just preach the Word because it will not return void."

Discussion Question: How would you respond to each of these objections to studying apologetics?

Christian Objections to Supporting Scripture with Evidence

- "We must believe Scripture's true because it says it's true or else you're 'testing Scripture' by another standard---and that's bad."

- "People won't repent no matter how much evidence you give them."

Discussion Question: How would you respond to each of these objections to supporting Scripture with evidence?

D. Christian Objections to Studying Apologetics

1. **Objection:** "People don't come to faith in Christ through apologetics."

   a. My discussion notes:

   a. People come to faith through the work of the

   _____ _____

   b. But there are _____ _____the Holy Spirit uses to do the work.

   c. One of them is apologetic _____.

2. **Objection:** "Don't give reasons to believe. Without faith, it's impossible to please God."

   a. My discussion notes:

   a. What's this mean?

      1) This implies evidence _____ the need for faith.

      2) But this comes from a misinterpretation of **Hebrews 11:6**. It's a misinterpretation based on an unbiblical definition of the word "faith."

   b. Biblical faith isn't a "_____ faith" that's opposed to reason, evidence or logic.

   c. 1 Cor. 15:12-19

3. **Objection:** "Don't give reasons to believe. Just preach the Word because it will not return void."

   a. My discussion notes:

   b. This comes from a misuse of **Isaiah 55:11**.

      1) The word "just" implies that _____else is needed in order for Scripture to begin its work in a person's heart.

      2) But Isaiah 55:11 _____ _____ include the word, "just."

c. Jesus and the apostles showed that other things could advance the gospel.

1) For example, they used miracles, godly lifestyle, prophecy, and reasoned argumentation to show the gospel message was true.

2) Peter and Jude's commands don't make sense if the only "_____ _____" of evangelism is directly preaching the gospel.

E. Christian Objections to Supporting Scripture with Evidence

1. **Objection:** "Don't give reasons to believe. We must believe Scripture's true because it says it's true or else you're 'testing Scripture' by another standard—and that's bad."

a. My discussion notes:

a. Some say that presenting evidence for the truth of Scripture means you are "judging" the text by a "more ultimate" standard. But what does the Bible itself teach about this?

    1) _____ used historical evidence to support God's word (1 Kings 18:20-45).

    2) Even God did not limit appeals to Scripture, but used historical evidence.[8]

        i. In Isaiah, God issued a challenge to false gods: Let them predict the future and make their predictions come true and prove they are gods (Is. 41:21-24; 44:7).

        ii. Turns out, only God can pass this test (Is. 41:25-29; 42:9; 44:24-28; 46:10; 48:5, 14).

        iii. The Jews were called to be witnesses of these historic events (Is. 44:6-8; 52:6).

---

[8] William Lane Craig, Gary Habermas and John Frame, eds., *Five Views on Apologetics*, ed. Steven B. Cowan (Grand Rapids, MI: Zondervan, 2000), 245.

3) _____ and _____ used
   historical evidence to support Jesus' words (Acts
   2:22-24, 16:30-31).

4) _____ used historical evidence to
   support His own claims (Matt. 11:4-5, Luke 7:18-
   23).

2. **Objection:** "People won't repent no matter how much
   evidence you give them."

   a. My discussion notes:

   b. **Matt. 11:20-21** shows that Jesus knows what would
      happen in any given circumstance, including people's free
      choices.

c. Remember that the Holy Spirit can use a variety of things to bring people to repentance including: A clear presentation of the gospel, a godly lifestyle, your personal testimony, *and* arguments and evidence, too.

1) There are _____

_____the Holy Spirit can use.

2) One of them is historical _____.

Works Cited

- Craig, William Lane, Gary Habermas, and John Frame, eds. *Five Views on Apologetics*. Edited by Steven B. Cowan. Grand Rapids, MI: Zondervan, 2000.

- Craig, William Lane. *Reasonable Faith: Christian Truth and Apologetics*. 3 ed. Wheaton: Crossway Books, 2008.

- Geisler, Norman L. *Baker Encyclopedia of Christian Apologetics (Baker Reference Library)*. Grand Rapids, MI: Baker Academic, 1998.

- Stott, John R.W. *Message of Ephesians: God's New Society (The Bible Speaks Today)*. New Ed ed. Downers Grove: Inter-Varsity Press, 1984.

- Thayer, and Smith. "Apologia - Greek Lexion." StudyLight.org. http://www.studylight.org/lex/grk/view.cgi?number=627 (accessed June 4, 2010).

- Zacharias, Ravi, William Dembski, Douglas Groothuis, Gary Habermas, Josh McDowell, Ben Witherington III, et al. *To Everyone an Answer: A Case for the Christian Worldview: Essays in Honor of Norman L. Geisler*. Edited by Francis J. Beckwith, William Lane Craig, James Porter Moreland and Norman L. Geisler. Downers Grove, Ill.: IVP Academic, 2004.

Introduction to Lesson 2

Lesson 2: Outline

Faith and Reason

I. Do Faith and Reason Mix?

II. How Do I Know Christianity is True?

III. How Can I Answer Objections to Truth?

Indiana Jones, Faith and Reason[9]

In the classic movie, *Indiana Jones and the Last Crusade*, there's a scene where Indy decides to take a "step of faith." He actually steps out into what looks like thin air in order to reach the Holy Grail.

It really seems crazy, but Indy follows the instructions in his father's diary and steps out anyway. He's totally surprised when his foot hits the ground. Turns out, there's actually a bridge across the cavern that he just couldn't see at first.[10]

---

[9] Tim Garrett, "Faith and Reason," Leadership U, http://www.leaderu.com/orgs/probe/docs/faithrea.html (accessed September 30, 2010).

[10] While playing the video game, *Lego Indiana Jones*, I discovered that this bridge is actually invisible in the Xbox 360 adaptation of this famous scene.

On the one hand, this scene seems to show how important it is to have faith. On the other, it seems to say that faith doesn't really make any sense. To Indy, taking that "step of faith" felt like giving up his better judgment, his intellect, and his reason. This tension is present in the church, too. But what about this? **Is the Christian faith actually opposed to reason?**

Tertullian, Athens and Jerusalem

A third-century thinker named Tertullian asked, "What indeed does Athens have to do with Jerusalem?"[11]

Here's his point: Philosophy, reason, and logic should have nothing to do with the church. Is he right? After all, didn't Paul warn us to be careful when dealing with philosophy? Check this out:

> "See to it that no one takes you captive through **hollow and deceptive philosophy**, which depends on human tradition and the basic principles of this world rather than on Christ."
>
> - **Paul, the Apostle** (Colossians 2:8 NIV)

---

[11] *On Prescription Against Heretics 7.*

Think about this: Some philosophies are empty, without substance, and totally deceptive; it's kind of like the façade of a Hollywood back lot or a bowl of plastic fruit. Some things look really good from far away, but they turn out to be fake when you take a closer look.

It's these *deceptive* philosophies that Paul was warning us about— ideas that are just based on traditions people made up instead of truth.

So he's not saying, "Don't study philosophy." Turns out, real philosophy goes hand-in-hand with good theology; Yes, philosophy can actually help us know more about God.

True, church fathers like Augustine, Luther and Calvin emphasized faith. But they knew that biblical faith isn't opposed to reason. Turns out, we actually *need* reason and logic in order to even understand the words of Scripture and investigate its truth claims.

As we begin this section of our study, keep in mind that **studying apologetics actually helps us identify philosophical deception, find out what's true and reject false ideas about God.**

Lesson 2:

How Do I Know Christianity Is True?

rea·son
(ree-zuhn) noun

1. a basis or cause, as for some belief, action, fact, event, etc.
2. a statement presented in justification or explanation of a belief or action.
3. **the mental powers concerned with forming conclusions, judgments, or inferences.**
4. **sound judgment; good sense.**
5. **normal or sound powers of mind; sanity.**

Dictionary.com Unabridged .Based on the Random House Dictionary, © Random House, Inc. 2010.

III.   Do Faith and Reason Mix?[12]

A. Faith and Belief

1. Let's look up the definition of the word, "reason."

2. **Question:** Imagine I asked you to "believe." Could you do it? Why not?

    a. We don't _____ "believe."

    b. We believe _____ something.

    c. To believe *in* something, like Christianity, means accepting a group of ideas as true.

    d. To do this, we've got to understand—at least on a certain level—the thing we're believing in (the object of our belief).

---

[12] Adapted from Steve Wilkens, *Good Ideas from Questionable Christians and Outright Pagans: An Introduction to Key Thinkers and Philosophies* (Downers Grove, Ill.: IVP Academic, 2004), 129-31

3. You can't _____ believing from _____.

4. That's why Greg Koukl says, "The mind is our first defense against error."[13]

5. Faith and reason aren't enemies at all.

6. We need _____ in order to have _____.

B. Faith and the Will

1. But having faith means more than just believing something's really true.

2. Even being sure of something requires another step before we get to faith.

    a. Faith means _____ like your belief is _____.

    b. This is an act of the will.

---

[13] Greg Koukl, *Tactics in Defending the Faith: Mentoring Audio.* Stand to Reason. Audio CD. 2003.

3. Beyond just agreeing that an idea is true, faith requires an act of the will.

    a. So, faith means trusting that our beliefs are actually true.

    b. But faith also means choosing to act on what we trust—and living like our beliefs are actually true.

C. The Relationship of Faith and Reason

1. Reason comes _____ _____ in that you need to understand what you're putting your faith in.

2. We've got to use our _____ to even be able to read the words in our Bibles, understand the gospel, and believe it's true.

3. But are reasonable arguments and evidence the basis of saving faith?

    i.   No. They aren't the basis of faith.
    ii. So what really convinces people that Christianity is true?
    iii. Let's talk about the difference between *knowing* and *showing* that Christianity is true.

IV.   How Do I Know Christianity is True?[14]

A. Knowing the Faith is True

    1. How do believers know that Christianity is true?

        a. It's ultimately the Holy Spirit that _____

        _____ that Christianity is true.

        b.   "The experience of the Holy Spirit is...unmistakable for him who has it; that such a person does not need supplementary arguments or evidence in order to know and to know with confidence that he is in fact experiencing the Spirit of God...(it) is the immediate experiencing of God himself."

        – William Lane Craig[15]

---

[14]Adapted from William Lane Craig, *Reasonable Faith: Christian Truth and Apologetics*, 3 ed. (Wheaton: Crossway Books, 2008), 31-50.
    [15] *Ibid.* 32.

c. Galatians 3:26; 4:6

d. Romans 8:16

e. John 14:16-17, 20

2. How do unbelievers come to know Christianity is true?

    a. It's ultimately the Holy Spirit that _____

        _____ that Christianity is true.

    b. John 16:7-11

    c. Romans 3:10-11

    d. John 6:44; 7:16-17

3. What is the role of argument and evidence?

    a. For believers, good arguments and historical evidences are just more confirmation that Christianity is really true.

    b. For unbelievers, the Holy Spirit may use arguments and evidences to draw people to Christ.

    c. If the witness of the Holy Spirit is the main way people know Christianity is true, any apologetic arguments or evidence will play a secondary role.

B. Showing the Faith is True

1. Let's contrast *knowing* Christianity is true with *showing* someone that it's true.

    a. Here, things are kind of reversed.

    b. We *know*—because of the Holy Spirit's witness—that Christianity is true.

    c. But how can we *show* an unbeliever that Christianity is true?

2. One of our roles is to _____   _____
    and evidences for Christian truth claims.

    a. Read Matt. 11:1-5

        1) How did Jesus respond to John's disciples?

        2) How is this an appeal to common ground?

    b. What are some examples of common ground we can use
        to begin showing that Christianity is true?

        1) We can use things everyone experiences in the world.

        2) We can even use something as basic as the laws of
            logic.

3. So, that's our role. What's the Holy Spirit's role?

4. The Holy Spirit's role is to _____ in the unbeliever's heart in such a way that he or she is

    _____ that Christianity is true.

III. Answering Objections to Truth[16]

A. Encountering Relativism

1. While you're talking about reasons to believe that Christianity is true, you might come across some objections to the very idea of **objective truth.**

2. One of our culture's main challenges to Christianity is relativism.

---

[16] Adapted from Paul Copan, *True for You, But Not for Me: Overcoming Objections to Christian Faith* (Minneapolis, Minn.: Bethany House, 1998), 23-38.

rel·a·tiv·ism

(rel-uh-tuh-viz-uhm) noun

A theory, especially in ethics or aesthetics, that conceptions of truth and moral values are not absolute but are relative to the persons or groups holding them.

The American Heritage® *Dictionary of the English Language*, Fourth Edition. Houghton Mifflin Company, 2010. Dictionary.com

a. Relativism is the idea that all truth claims are just opinions.

b. Relativism is the belief that _____ _____ does not exist.

3. But many relativistic slogans turn out to be

_____ - _____

4. How do relativists show that they really believe in objective truth?

B. A conversational tactic for apologists[17]

1. Begin by _____   _____

    a.   "...being an asker allows you control of situations that statement-makers rarely achieve. Once you learn how to guide a conversation, you have also learned to control it." —Hugh Hewitt[18]

    b. Jesus used this method

        i.   Lk. 20:22-26

        ii.   Lk. 20:4

---

[17] Adapted from Greg Koukl's article, "Applying Apologetics to Everyday Life" in *To Everyone an Answer.*

[18] *In, But Not Of*, p.173. Cited in the above, P.49.

c. Three goals of asking a question

    i.   To gain _____

    ii. To _____ the burden of proof

    iii. To _____ a weakness in a view or position

2. Three kinds of questions:

a. Get more info: "What do you _____ by that?"

b. Ask for proof: "How did you come to that _____?"

c. Expose the Flaw: "Have you ever _____ the idea that..."

Responding to relativistic slogans:

- "You shouldn't try to convert people to your views."
- "Christians are intolerant of other viewpoints."
- "That's true for you but not for me."

Discussion Question: How would you respond to each of these relativistic slogans?

C. Responding to Relativistic Slogans

1. **Slogan:** "You shouldn't try to convert people to your views."

2. **Slogan:** "Christians are intolerant of other viewpoints."

3. **Slogan:** "That's true for you but not for me."

Works Cited

Copan, Paul. *True for You, But Not for Me: Overcoming Objections to Christian Faith*. Minneapolis, Minn.: Bethany House, 1998.

Craig, William Lane. *Reasonable Faith: Christian Truth and Apologetics*. 3 ed. Wheaton: Crossway Books, 2008.

Garrett, Tim. "Faith and Reason." Leadership U. http://www.leaderu.com/orgs/probe/docs/faithrea.html (accessed September 30, 2010).

Koukl, Greg. *Tactics in Defending the Faith: Mentoring Audio. Stand to Reason*. Audio CD. 2003.

Ratiner, Tracie, ed. *Encyclopedia of World Biography.* 2nd ed. Detroit: Gale Virtual Reference Library, 2007. http://go.galegroup.com.ezproxy.apollolibrary.com/ps/i.do?&id=GALE%7C CX2699800032&v=2.1&u=uphoenix&it=r&p=GVRL&sw=w (accessed June 19, 2010).

Wilkens, Steve. *Good Ideas from Questionable Christians and Outright Pagans: An Introduction to Key Thinkers and Philosophies*. Downers Grove, Ill.: IVP Academic, 2004.

Introduction to Lesson 3

> ## Outline
>
> ### Lesson 3: Evidence for God
>
> I. Is God Real?
>
> II. Why Does God Allow Evil?

A Dead Guy's Facebook Profile

Early one morning, I was on my computer and got a Facebook alert. It looked like one of my friends had a birthday coming up. But here's what Facebook didn't know: The guy had been dead for almost a year.

A dead guy's Facebook profile is an eerie thing. We went to the same high school, although I really didn't know him that well. His profile picture is still the same. His status hadn't been updated since June 26, 2009. His last post: "Just saying, best night ever."

It was a sobering reminder of our own mortality. What will be left of us after we die? An abandoned Facebook page listing all your influential friends? A pile of money in the bank? Other symbols of success we spent our every waking moment trying to achieve? Is this really all there is?

Imagine there's No Heaven

John Lennon envisioned a utopia that didn't need the idea of heaven or God.[19] But what if there was no afterlife? Even worse, what if there was no God? Would it really change anything?

Think about it like this: If God isn't real, then you, me, every single one of your friends, family members, and the world we live in is basically an accident. We're basically what happens when you throw stuff, time and chance into mix. There's no reason we're even alive.

Who cares if you had 2,000 Facebook friends? Who cares if you were the most popular kid in school? If you landed that great job? Or if you had the coolest car or biggest house? This can really get you depressed. If God isn't real, we're just sitting around waiting to die.

There are huge implications to the very first verse of the Bible:

> "In the beginning, God created the heavens and the earth."
> **Genesis 1:1 (NIV)**

Here's how God makes a difference: If God is real, your life has real meaning. You are not an accident. If God exists, this life is not all there is. But even more than this, if *Christianity* is true, eternal life with God is possible and available to you. Are there any good reasons to believe that God is real?

---

[19] Bob Passantino and Gretchen Passantino, "Imagine there's no Heaven," *Christian Research Journal* 22, no. 3 (2000). http://www.equip.org/articles/imagine-there-s-no-heaven (accessed November 10, 2010).

Lesson 3:

Is God Real?

I. Is God Real?

A. Why Ask This Question?

1. It's a _____   _____.

    a. The way a person answers this question affects a person's answer to the question, "What is the meaning of life?"

    b. If God is _____ _____, life has no real

    _____.

    c. Helping someone think through this question can help them move closer to a belief in God.

2. There's a _____ _____.

    a. There are only two possibilities:

    b. There are good reasons to believe that God is real.

    c. **If God is _____, life has real _____.**

    d. The Bible assumes that God is real right from the get-go (Genesis 1:1).

    e. But there *are* arguments for the existence of God based on our common experience in this world (Psalm 19:1).

B. Three Arguments for the Existence of God

    1. Let's take a look at three key arguments based on:

        a. The existence of the _____

        b. The existence of _____in the universe

        c. The existence of objective _____ values

    2. Together, these arguments help build a good case for the existence of God.

C. An Argument Based on the Existence of the Universe[20]

    1. **Big idea:** God is the best explanation for why the universe exists.

    2. The first part of the argument goes like this:

        a. Whatever _____ to exits has a

        _____.

---

[20] Much of my presentation is generally adapted from material I learned directly from William Lane Craig and J.P. Moreland. For an in depth treatment, see: William Lane Craig, *On Guard: Defending Your Faith with Reason and Precision*, New ed. (Wheaton: David C. Cook, 2010), 53-65 and 73-104. For a more condensed treatment, see William Lane Craig, "The Craig-Washington Debate: Dr. Craig's Opening Arguments," Leadership University, http://www.leaderu.com/offices/billcraig/docs/washdeba-craig1.html (accessed August 7, 2010).

b. The _____   _____ to exist.

    i. Evidence for the Big Bang shows the universe is not eternal, but had a beginning.[21]

        1) This means that the universe was created *out of nothing.*

        2) This seems to line up well with what Christians already believe: That God created the universe *out of nothing.*

        3) Genesis 1:1

        4) John 1:3

        5) Hebrews 11:3

    ii. So if whatever begins to exist has a cause

    iii. And if the universe began to exist

    iv. We know that…

---

[21] You don't need to believe the Big Bang Theory is accurate to understand or use this argument with someone who does not believe God created the universe. Most atheists hold to some version of the Big Bang Theory. Even on this view, the universe still had a beginning which requires a cause.

c. The universe has a _____.

    i. There's got to be a _____
    _____ that started it all.

    ii. **Illustration 1:** At the bookstore

        1. Draw something to remind you of this illustration:

        2. Just like this, there's got to be a first event in the chain.

        3. And that first event has a first cause.

iii. **Illustration 2:** In the classroom[22]

    1. Draw something to remind you of this illustration:

    2. Existence is like this, too.

    3. At the end of the chain, you've got to end up with someone who has always been there.

    4. Everything that exists actually owes its existence to this First Cause.

iv. The First Cause has to be_____,

_____ and _____ a physical kind of thing.

---

[22] Adapted from J.P. Moreland's verbal illustration of the argument using the question, "Can I borrow an iPod?" in *Responding to the New Atheism*. Volume 1. Biola University Lecture CD.

2. The next part helps us figure out if the cause of the universe is personal or not:

   a. If the universe was caused, the cause has got to be either:

      i. An impersonal thing

      ii. Or personal being

      iii. If it's an impersonal thing, like eternal conditions, we would have an eternal effect.

      iv. But we already know the universe isn't eternal.

      v. It makes more sense to consider the idea of a personal being—an unmoved mover—who freely chose to create the universe.

   b. This kind of personal being is what most people mean by the word "God."

D. Argument Based on Design Seen in the Universe

1. **Big Idea:** God is the best explanation for things that look designed in the world.

2. "The theory of intelligent design holds that certain features of the universe and of living things are best explained by an intelligent cause, not an undirected process such as natural selection."[23]

---

[23] "Intelligent Design," Explaining the Science of Intelligent Design, http://www.intelligentdesign.org/whatisid.php (accessed October 15, 2010).

3. We find some awesome examples of intelligent design in the universe.

    a. What are some examples of things you see in nature that look like they were designed?

    b. List your top three examples.

        1.

        2.

        3.

    c. Coded, instructional _____in DNA

        i. **Drawing Time:**
            a. Draw a DNA double-helix

            b. Write the letters A, T, G and C to represent the nucleotide bases: adenine, thymine, guanine, and cytosine.

ii.   The way these letters are set up have a lot in common with the way letters in a book make up words and sentences.[24]

iii.   The order of these nucleotide bases (A, T, G, & C) works just like a secret _____ or the letters in a book.

iv.   The late British Philosopher Anthony Flew—a former atheist—said that the best arguments of the existence of God came from science: "It now seems to me that the findings of more than fifty years of DNA research have provided materials for a new and enormously powerful argument to design." [25]

---

[24] William Dembski and James Kushiner, eds., *Signs of Intelligence: Understanding Intelligent Design*, 1st ed. (Grand Rapids: Brazos Press, 2001), 108.

[25] Gary Habermas and Anthony Flew, "Atheist Becomes Theist," *Philosophia Christi* (09 Decemebr 2004): page nr., http://www.biola.edu/antonyflew/page2.cfm (accessed November 10, 2010). See also: Antony Flew and Roy Abraham Varghese, *There Is a God: How the World's Most Notorious Atheist Changed His Mind*, 1st Reprint ed. (San Francisco, Calif.: HarperOne, 2007).

4. Instructional information implies an _____.

5. Encoded information implies an _____.

6. An information processing system implies a _____.

7. The intelligent design was see in nature tells us about the existence of a powerful intelligent designer: God.

objective

(uhb-jek-tiv) adjective

1. existing independently of perception or an individual's conceptions (e.g *are there objective moral values?*)

2. undistorted by emotion or personal bias

3. of or relating to actual and external phenomena as opposed to thoughts, feelings, etc.

Dictionary.com Unabridged. Based on the Collins English Dictionary, © HarperCollins Publishers. 2003.

E. Argument Based on Objective Moral Values

1. **Big Idea:** God is the best explanation for objective moral values in the world.

   a. This argument infers the existence of God from the existence of objective moral laws that we all know about in the world.

   b. Romans 2:15

c. If God doesn't exist, would *objective* moral values exist?

2. First, if morality is just something we made up or something that evolved over time, it wouldn't be *objective*.

3. Second, if God isn't real, then what's so special about people?

4. But objective moral values do exist and we all know it.

5. Where do moral laws come from?

    a. Moral laws have an "_____" to
        them.

    b. Moral laws are the _____ of
        _____.

    c. Moral laws imply the existence of a Moral _____
        _____.

II. Why Does God Allow Evil?

A. Defining the Problem

1. This is one of the most common reasons people give for believing that God isn't real.

2. Here's one way to make the implication a lot clearer:[26]

   a. If God is all-powerful, He _____ destroy evil

   b. If God is all-good, He _____d destroy evil

   c. But evil is _____ destroyed

   d. So, a God like this probably doesn't exist.[27]

---

[26] Adapted from Norman L. Geisler and Ronald M. Brooks, *When Skeptics Ask: A Handbook on Christian Evidences* (Grand Rapids: Baker Books, 1990), 63.

[27] Thoughtful atheists don't try to say, "God can't exist in a world where evil exists" anymore. Why? Because as long as it's even possible for God to have a good reason for allowing evil and suffering, the "logical problem of evil" (as philosophers call it) has been solved. But even if that's *possible*, critics can still say that it's pretty *improbable* or *unlikely* that an all-powerful, all-good God is real.

4. When you think about all the suffering and evil things people do to each other, it does make it pretty tough to believe that God is real.

5. But is that the only piece of evidence we have to look at?

B. Thinking about Evil

1. What *is* evil?

    a. How would you define it?

    b. Evil shows up in two ways:

        i.   Moral evil

        ii.   Natural evil

    c. If objective moral laws are real, there's got to be an objective moral lawgiver.

        i. C.S. Lewis said, "My argument against God was that the universe seemed so cruel and unjust. But how had I got this idea of *just* and *unjust?* A man does not call a line crooked unless he has some idea of a straight line." [28]

        ii. Objective moral laws don't just come out of nowhere.

2. Why is there evil and suffering in our world?

    a. We have a real _____ about what we do.

    b. Moral freedom gives us two things:

        i. The ability to_____

        ii. The possibility of _____

        iii. God made evil _____, but people made evil _____.

---

[28] C. S. Lewis, *Mere Christianity: Comprising The Case for Christianity, Christian Behaviour, and Beyond Personality.* New York: Touchstone, 1996. 45.

3. How can we rethink the problem of evil?

    a. Just because God has _____ _____ removed evil from the world, doesn't mean he never will.

    b. Norman Geisler restates the problem of evil like this:[29]

        i.   If God is all-powerful, He _____ defeat evil.

        ii.   If God is all-good, He _____ defeat evil

        iii. Evil is not _____ defeated.

        iv.   So, God can and will one day defeat evil.

_____

[29] *When Skeptics Ask*, 64-65.

C. Evil as Evidence for God

1. Three things we know about morality:

    a. Moral laws are real

    b. Moral laws are a kind of communication

        i.   Laws are _____.

        ii.   This implies the existence of at least two minds.

2. Where did moral laws come from?

D. Answering the Problem of Evil

1. Moral evil exists because free creatures freely choose to do immoral things.

2. Immoral actions imply moral laws.

3. Moral laws imply a moral _____ _____.

4. His laws tell us what He wants us to do—and He expects us to obey.

5. The moral law and the problem of evil are evidence for the existence of God.

Works Cited

Craig, William Lane. *On Guard: Defending Your Faith with Reason and Precision.* New ed. Wheaton: David C. Cook, 2010.

Craig, William Lane. *Reasonable Faith: Christian Truth and Apologetics.* 3 ed. Wheaton: Crossway Books, 2008.

Craig, William Lane. "The Craig-Washington Debate: Dr. Craig's Opening Arguments." Leadership University. http://www.leaderu.com/offices/billcraig/docs/washdeba-craig1.html (accessed August 7, 2010).

Dembski, William, and James Kushiner, eds. *Signs of Intelligence: Understanding Intelligent Design.* 1St Edition ed. Grand Rapids: Brazos Press, 2001.

Flew, Antony, and Roy Abraham Varghese. *There Is a God: How the World's Most Notorious Atheist Changed His Mind.* 1 Reprint ed. San Francisco, Calif.: HarperOne, 2007.

Geisler, Norman L., and Ronald M. Brooks. *When Skeptics Ask: A Handbook on Christian Evidences.* Grand Rapids: Baker Books, 1990.

Habermas, Gary, and Anthony Flew. "Atheist Becomes Theist." *Philosophia Christi* (09 Decemebr 2004): page nr. http://www.biola.edu/antonyflew/page2.cfm (accessed November 10, 2010).

"Intelligent Design." Explaining the Science of Intelligent Design. http://www.intelligentdesign.org/whatisid.php (accessed October 15, 2010).

Lewis, C. S. *Mere Christianity: Comprising The Case for Christianity, Christian Behaviour, and Beyond Personality.* New York: Touchstone, 1996. 45.

Passantino, Bob, and Gretchen Passantino. "Imagine there's no Heaven." *Christian Research Journal* 22, no. 3 (2000). http://www.equip.org/articles/imagine-there-s-no-heaven (accessed November 10, 2010).

Introduction to Lesson 4

Lesson Outline

Fact or Fiction

I. Did God Speak to Us?

II. Can I Trust My Bible?

III. Questions and Conspiracies

The Blind Men and the Elephant[30]

Have you ever heard the parable of the Blind Men and the Elephant? It's a common story that's often told in Religious Studies courses. In fact, while teaching a World Religious Traditions course at University of Phoenix, I discovered this passage in our textbook:[31]

A famous story illustrates the relativity of truth. Several blind men touch the same elephant but experience it quite differently. The first man touches the ear and says it is a fan; the second man touches the leg and says it is a tree trunk; the third man touches the tail and says it is a rope; and so on.

But something's missing. Something important.

---

[30] Adapted from *Christianity and the Challenge of World Religions*, Craig Hazen's lecture at Bayside Christian Church in Granite Bay, CA (August 28, 2010). See also: Ed Hindson and Ergun Caner, *The Popular Encyclopedia of Apologetics: Surveying the Evidence for the Truth of Christianity* (Eugene: Harvest House Publishers, 2008), 430.

[31] Michael Molloy, *Experiencing the World's Religions*, 5 ed. (New York: McGraw-Hill Humanities/Social Sciences/Languages, 2009), 196.

If you go back to the earliest rendition of this traditional story, you'll find that it doesn't illustrate the relativity of truth at all. In fact, it turns out to be quite the opposite.

Here's the complete story: There's an elephant in the middle of a courtyard that belongs to a *rajah* or a king. A bunch of blind men do walk into the courtyard, bump into the elephant, and start saying they've bumped into all sorts of different things. Then, these guys actually get into a fist fight, arguing over who's right!

Now, this is where many people stop and begin to say that all religious traditions grab on to different parts of reality and interpret their experiences in different ways. And to some extent, it's true that we're all involved in some kind of blindness, trying to make sense of our world. But does that mean no one can claim to know the truth? The story doesn't end here.

This is the original ending of the parable—the part that's often left out of the Religious Studies textbooks: The king, or the *rajah*, steps out onto his balcony and looks down at these guys in the courtyard. Then, he speaks to them and solves the mystery: "Listen, you foolish blind men. You are all touching the same thing. You are all touching the elephant."

Tell It Like It Is

Here's the point: The king, or the *rajah*, sees the situation as it really is. And he spoke to the blind men so they could know what was really going on.

Remember that Keanu Reeves film, *The Matrix*? This is kind of like when Morpheus told Neo that he was unknowingly enslaved by a computer-generated simulation, called the Matrix. This is the kind of thing our world is looking for—a message from someone who can see the world objectively and tell it like it is. We need a word from above.

Even the great philosophers like Plato longed for something like this: "If only I had a raft of revelation to carry me over the seas of doubt."[32] Is it possible that we've received that word from above? Has God spoken to us?

The Bible is a collection of ancient documents written by people who say that God has given us that word from above. But more than this, the Scriptures claim to be the actual words of God:

All Scripture is God-breathed and is useful for teaching, rebuking, correcting and training in righteousness, so that the man of God may be thoroughly equipped for every good work.

- **Paul, the apostle** (2 Timothy 3:16-17 NIV)

Is the Bible fact or fiction? Can I trust the Bible I'm reading today?

---

[32] *Phaedo*, cited in Craig J. Hazen, *Five Sacred Crossings: A Novel Approach to a Reasonable Faith* (ConversantLife.com®) (Eugene: Harvest House Publishers, 2008), 144.

Lesson 4:

Can I Trust My Bible?

objective

*(uhb-**jek**-tiv) adjective*

1. existing independently of perception or an individual's conceptions (e.g *are there objective moral values?*)

2. undistorted by emotion or personal bias

3. of or relating to actual and external phenomena as opposed to thoughts, feelings, etc.

Dictionary.com Unabridged. Based on the Collins English Dictionary, © HarperCollins Publishers. 2003.

I. Did God Speak to Us?

A. We need more than _____.

1. Many people have religious experiences they can talk about.

2. But religious experiences can be used to support all kinds of claims:

   a. Mormons

   b. Jehovah's Witnesses

   c. Betty Eadie

3. How do we know which "Jesus" is the *real* Jesus?

4. We need an _____ authority.

B. We've only got two options.

1. Think about it in terms of cause and effect:

   a. The Bible is an effect.

   b. What caused it?

   c. We've only got two options here.

2. Option One: It's *just* ideas about God, _____ by people.

3. Option Two: It's actually the Word of God,

   _____ to people.

4. The Bible *claims* to be God's message to us.

   a. Hundreds of times, you read things like "God actually *said*

      this!"[33]

   b. The words the writers wrote down are also called the words of God; Even between the Old and New Testaments, you read that "Scripture says this" equals "God says this."[34]

   c. 2 Tim 3:16-17

---

[33] See Exodus 4:12, 20:1, Isaiah 59:21, and Hebrews 1:1.
[34] See Genesis 12:1-3 and Galatians 3:8.

C. Three Signs of the Supernatural

1. Its _____.

2. Its _____.

    a. Prophecies that came true about _____ [35]

      i. Isaiah 53:2-12

      ii. Jesus fulfilled them all (Matthew 26-27, Mark 15-16, Luke 22-23, John 18-19)

---

[35] Norman L. Geisler, *Baker Encyclopedia of Christian Apologetics* (Baker Reference Library) (Grand Rapids, MI: Baker Academic, 1998), 611.

b. Prophecies that came true about _____ [36]

   i. Isaiah 11:11-16

   ii. This second return happened when Israel became a unified nation in 1948.

3. It's _____ _____!

II. Can I Trust My Bible?

A. How reliable is your Bible?

1. A Book of Ancient History:

---

[36] *Ibid.* 613.

2. Ancient Document Rule[37]

    a. Federal Rules of Evidence

    b. Interestingly, Harvard Law Professor Simon Greenleaf
        argued that you could submit the New Testament Gospels as
        evidence in a court of law—and this guy literally wrote the
        book on legal evidence used in American law schools during
        the 19th century![38]

3. The Bible is very reliable. Most English translations of the Bible
    are _____ _____ to the original
    documents.

---

[37] "Ancient Document Rule | LII/ Legal Information Institute," Cornell University Law School, http://topics.law.cornell.edu/wex/ancient_document_rule (accessed November 17, 2010).

[38] See: Simon Greenleaf, *The Testimony of the Evangelists: The Gospels Examined by the Rules of Evidence* (Grand Rapids, MI: Kregel Classics, 1995).

B. The Old Testament[39]

1. All the manuscripts _____.

   a. The English Bible you have today was translated *directly* from the best, earliest manuscripts historians have discovered.

   b. Even if you don't read Hebrew, try this:

      i. View the Hebrew text of Isaiah 1:1 [40]

      חזון ישעיהו בן־אמוץ אשר חזה על־יהודה וירושלם בימי עזיהו יותם אחז יחזקיהו מלכי יהודה:

      ii. View the Great Isaiah Scroll online: http://www.apologeticsguy.com/isaiahscroll [41]

      iii. Note: Hebrew is written from right to left, so you'll have to scroll all the way to the right to find chapter 1.

      iv. Anyone can look at this ancient document and compare the text.

      v. Now you can say you've actually seen it for yourself!

---

[39] For a more detailed treatment, see Norman Geisler and William Nix, *General Introduction to the Bible*, Rev Exp Su ed. (Chicago: Moody Publishers, 1986), 249-66.

[40] Taken from http://unbound.biola.edu. Select "Hebrew OT: WLC (Consonants Only)" and "Isaiah 1" to see more of this. If you want to know how to read this, see the interlinear here: http://interlinearbible.org/isaiah/1.htm

[41] This easy-to-remember link forwards to "The Dorot Foundation Dead Sea Scrolls Information and Study Center," The Israel Museum, Jerusalem, http://www.imj.org.il/shrine_center/Isaiah_Scrolling/index.html (accessed November 17, 2010).

2. These also agree with the

   _____ [42]

3. These also agree with the _____ _____

   _____

   a. For example, two copies of Isaiah discovered in the caves "proved to be word for word identical with our standard Hebrew Bible in more than 95 percent of the text."[43]

   b. The rest (5%) was mostly made up of differences in spelling or other variations that don't change the meaning of any piece of doctrine or theology.[44]

4. A major reason for this consistency is that Jewish copyists were

   _____!

5. They followed a strict code when copying Scripture:[45]

6. Because of this, nobody's ever discovered a major change in the text.

7. Your English translation of the Old Testament is a very good representation of the original manuscripts.

---

[42] This is a 2nd-3rd century BC Greek translation of the Old Testament.

[43] Gleason Archer, *A Survey of Old Testament Introduction* (Chicago: Moody Publishers, 2007), 19.

[44] *Ibid.* 25.

[45] Adapted from *Baker Encyclopedia of Christian Apologetics*, 552.

C. The New Testament

1. **Objection:** "The Bible's been copied and translated so many times that we can't be sure what the originals said."

2. Many people don't understand the way the Bible was copied and translated.

    a. Bible translators don't translate a translation of a translation.

    b. Again, the English Bible you have today was translated *directly* from the best, earliest manuscripts historians have discovered.

    c. Your Bible has only been translated _____!

3. The way the New Testament was copied isn't anything like the telephone game.[46]

4. It's easier to get to the original message when you're dealing with documents.

---

[46] Adapted from Greg Koukl, "Stand To Reason: Is the New Testament Text Reliable?" *Stand to Reason*, http://www.str.org/site/News2?page=NewsArticle&id=6068 (accessed November 18, 2010).

5. People who study books of ancient history for a living love to find a lot of manuscripts written pretty close to the originals.

    a. Homer's *Illiad*: 643 ancient copies.[47]

    b. Julius Caesar's *Gallic Wars:* 10 ancient copies; the earliest one was made 1,000 years after the original.[48]

    c. New Testament: _____ Greek manuscripts![49]

    d. Some of these ancient copies of the New Testament were written within 70 years of the originals!

6. We have 100% of the New Testament text and we're sure of over _____% of it.

7. Most variants are differences in _____ or word

    _____ and not one changes the meaning of an essential doctrine or theology.

8. Your English translation of the New Testament is a very good representation of the original manuscripts.

---

[47] *Ibid.*
[48] *Ibid.*
[49] *Ibid.*

III. Questions and Conspiracies

A. Are There Any Missing Books of the Bible? [50]

1. Our four gospel accounts were put together in one collection at an early date.

    a. **125 AD:** Aristides

    b. **170 AD:** Tatian

    c. **180 AD:** Irenaeus

2. But the church had to let people know which books contained Jesus' real teachings.

    a. **140 AD:** Marcion[51]

---

[50] F.F. Bruce, "The Canon of the New Testament," Bible Research, http://www.bible-researcher.com/bruce1.html (accessed November 18, 2010).

[51] Marcion was whack. He rejected the Old Testament and only accepted certain New Testament writings ---and only after his own personal edits to them! See also: "The Development of the Canon of the New Testament," http://www.ntcanon.org/Marcion.shtml (accessed November 18, 2010).

    b. The church had to guard the original teachings of Jesus and the apostles by letting everyone know which documents really represented Christianity.

3. **F.F. Bruce observed:** "The New Testament books did not become authoritative for the Church because they were formally included in a canonical list; on the contrary, the Church included them in her canon because she already regarded them as divinely inspired, recognizing their innate worth and general apostolic authority, direct or indirect. The first ecclesiastical councils to classify the canonical books were both held in North Africa — at Hippo Regius in 393 and at Carthage in 397 — but what these councils did was not to impose something new upon the Christian communities but to codify what was already the general practice of those communities."[52]

---

[52] F.F. Bruce. "The Canon of the New Testament"

4. How do we know that our Bible isn't missing any other books?[53]

    a. **Think about it like this:** There's only two ways to view the Bible:

        i.   Supernatural view

        ii. Naturalistic view

    b. "It's impossible, rationally—nothing to do with spiritual commitments at all —that there can be anything like lost books of the Bible." – Greg Koukl.[54]

B. What about the Apocrypha?[55]

1. The Apocrypha is a collection of books found in a number of Greek translations of the Old Testament.

2. The Catholic church canonized these in 1546 at the Council of Trent after Martin Luther asked the church to give a biblical reason for Catholic traditions like praying for the dead (this shows up in Tobit 12:9).

---

[53] Adapted from Koukl, Greg. "No Lost Books of the Bible." Stand to Reason. http://www.str.org/site/News2?page=NewsArticle&id=5473 (accessed November 18, 2010).
[54] *Ibid.*
[55] Adapted from Norman L. Geisler and Ronald M. Brooks, *When Skeptics Ask: A Handbook on Christian Evidences* (Grand Rapids: Baker Books, 1990), 155-156.

C. What about the Gnostic Gospels?[56]

1. Gnostic works like the *Gospel of Thomas* and the *Gospel of Judas* are part of the *pseudepigrapha*.

2. *Pseudepigrapha* means "false writings."

D. Was the Bible changed at the Council of Nicea?[57]

1. Dan Brown's novel, *The Da VinciCode*, gives the impression that the Bible was changed and Jesus' divinity was made up by Constantine at the Council of Nicea.

2. According to people who were actually at the Council of Nicea, Eusebius and Athanasius, Christ's deity was the reason for meeting, **not** the result of it.

   i. Constantine called the council which met from June 14 to July 25, 325 A.D.

   ii. 318 bishops showed up with two presbyters each.

---

[56] *Ibid.* 156-157.
[57] Greg Koukl, *The Da Vinci Code Cracks* (Signal HIll: Stand to Reason, 2006), http://www.str.org/site/DocServer/5-6_2006_SG.pdf?docID=961 (accessed November 18, 2010).

3. References to Jesus divinity are all over writings from the first three centuries—even Gnostic works.

   i. In the Brown's novel, Jesus' divinity was the result of a very close vote.

   ii. In reality, when the question came up about Jesus' divinity, only 2 out of 318 bishops sided with Arius.

4. The books of the New Testament were not an issue at the Council of Nicea.

5. There's no good reason to think the New Testament changed over time through endless translations, sneaky revisions or outright tampering.

6. Instead, the historical evidence tells us it's the most reliable collection of ancient documents the world has ever seen.

Works Cited

"Ancient Document Rule | LII/ Legal Information Institute." Cornell University Law School. http://topics.law.cornell.edu/wex/ancient_document_rule (accessed November 17, 2010).

Archer, Gleason. *A Survey of Old Testament Introduction*. Chicago: Moody Publishers, 2007.

"Dorot Foundation Dead Sea Scrolls Information and Study Center." The Israel Museum, Jerusalem. http://www.imj.org.il/shrine_center/Isaiah_Scrolling/index.html (accessed November 17, 2010).

Bruce, F.F. "The Canon of the New Testament." Bible Research. http://www.bible-researcher.com/bruce1.html (accessed November 18, 2010).

Geisler, Norman L. *Baker Encyclopedia of Christian Apologetics* (Baker Reference Library). Grand Rapids, MI: Baker Academic, 1998.

——— and William Nix. *General Introduction to the Bible*. Rev Exp Su ed. Chicago: Moody Publishers, 1986.

———, and Ronald M. Brooks. *When Skeptics Ask: A Handbook on Christian Evidences*. Grand Rapids: Baker Books, 1990.

Greenleaf, Simon. *The Testimony of the Evangelists: The Gospels Examined by the Rules of Evidence*. Grand Rapids, MI.: Kregel Classics, 1995.

Hazen, Craig J. *Five Sacred Crossings: A Novel Approach to a Reasonable Faith* (ConversantLife.com®). Eugene: Harvest House Publishers, 2008.

Hindson, Ed, and Ergun Caner. *The Popular Encyclopedia of Apologetics: Surveying the Evidence for the Truth of Christianity.* Eugene: Harvest House Publishers, 2008.

Koukl, Greg. "The Da Vinci Code Cracks." Signal HIll: Stand to Reason, 2006. http://www.str.org/site/DocServer/5-6_2006_SG.pdf?docID=961 (accessed November 18, 2010).

——— "Is The New Testament Text Reliable?" Stand to Reason. http://www.str.org/site/News2?page=NewsArticle&id=6068 (accessed November 18, 2010).

——— "No Lost Books of the Bible," Stand to Reason. http://www.str.org/site/News2?page=NewsArticle&id=5473 (accessed November 18, 2010).

Molloy, Michael. *Experiencing the World's Religions.* 5 ed. New York: McGraw-Hill Humanities/Social Sciences/Languages, 2009.

Introduction to Lesson 5

> # Lesson 5: Outline
>
> **Dead or Alive**
>
> I. Making history
>
> II. Did Jesus rise from the dead?

The Strangest Passage in Religion

Let me introduce this section by sharing something Dr. Craig Hazen calls "the strangest passage in all of religious literature."[58] It's not some magic spell supposedly hidden by the ancient Pharaohs. It's not a vision in the *Bhagavad Gita* or an exotic ritual from the *Tibetan Book of the Dead*. It's actually something the Apostle Paul wrote in a letter to the church in Corinth.

"If Jesus has not been raised, your faith is worthless; you are still under condemnation for your sins. In that case, all who have died believing in Christ have perished."

- Paul, the Apostle (1 Corinthians 15:17-18 NIV)

---

[58] *Christianity and the Challenge of World Religions*, Public lecture at Bayside Christian Church in Granite Bay, CA (August 28, 2010).

This is pretty unique claim in world religions. Why is this so strange?

Because Paul did something huge when he wrote this—something you won't find in any other religious text: **He pinned the validity of the entire Christian faith on a historical event that either happened or didn't happen.**

Paul's basically saying, "If Jesus didn't really rise from the dead, Christianity is a total lie." He goes on to say that if Jesus didn't really rise from the dead, he and all the other apostles are liars, too. And if this is the case, everyone who believes in Jesus still owes God for their sins. That's pretty serious. But the opposite is also true. If Jesus really rose from the dead, this historic event shows that he was actually telling the truth. Jesus is the Messiah. Christianity is true.

I Saw the Sign

Don't forget how Paul was a former enemy of the faith who quit his prestigious job and willingly endured all kinds of suffering because he says he saw Jesus alive after this public execution.

When the Pharisees and teachers of the law asked Jesus for a sign that what he was saying was true, he said he would give them one: The resurrection.

> "A wicked and adulterous generation asks for a miraculous sign! But none will be given it except the sign of the prophet Jonah. For as Jonah was three days and three nights in the belly of a huge fish, so the Son of Man will be three days and three nights in the heart of the earth."
>
> **- Jesus, the Messiah** (Matthew 12:18 NIV)

This is totally different from the kinds of subjective truth-tests we find other religions. For example, a Mormon could say she read the *Book of Mormon*, prayed, and God gave her a "burning in the bosom" to prove that Mormonism is true. But what about those who haven't received these warm feelings?

It seems like everyone's got spiritual experiences they can tell you about. Christianity is different because Jesus' resurrection is objective. Either he really rose from the dead or he is a fake and a total liar. Part of the reason that Paul's words are so unique in religious literature is that the resurrection of Jesus is something that can be investigated historically.

Body of Evidence

Remember that the main way we know Christianity is true is because of the Holy Spirit's witness (Romans 8:16). But Jesus' resurrection confirms that the confidence we have is really from God. Think about it like this: If a Christian and a non-Christian both say their religion is true, we've got an objective test. If Jesus really rose from the dead, Christianity is true.

But can we really prove Jesus' resurrection historically? Depends what you mean by proof...

plausible
(plaw-zuh-buhl) adjective

having an appearance of truth or reason; seemingly worthy of approval or acceptance; credible; believable: *a plausible excuse; a plausible plot.*

Dictionary.com Unabridged. Based on the *Random House Dictionary*, © Random House, Inc. 2010.

I. Making History[59]

A. How we know that past events really happened

1. When it comes to history, having "proof" doesn't mean it's impossible to be wrong.

2. In studying history, you deal with "_____ of certainty."

3. In a court of law, you deal with something called

    "_____."

4. What kinds of evidence support historical claims really well? Here are five of them

---

[59] Adapted from Gary R. Habermas and Michael Licona, *The Case for the Resurrection of Jesus* (Grand Rapids, MI: Kregel Publications, 2004), 36-40.

B. Five types of evidence that help make history

1. Reports from _____ than one

    _____ source.

2. Reports that make the witness or their friends _____

    _____.

3. Reports from an _____.

4. Reports from an _____.

5. Reports that are _____.

II.   Five Historical Facts

A. The "_____ _____"
Approach[60]

1. This approach only uses facts that most historians—both Christians and non-Christians—actually agree on.

2. The strategy is to say that the Resurrection of Jesus is the best explanation for these historical facts.

3. Again, we're only mentioning historical evidence that pretty much every scholar who studies the reported Resurrection of Jesus will agree on—even the rather skeptical ones.[61]

B. The Benefits of This Approach

1. You don't have to deal with objections like "Well, the Bible is full of errors, so we can't know that Jesus rose from the dead."

2. Even if someone rejects the Bible as God's Word, they still have to deal with the historical facts.

---

[60] I learned this approach from Gary Habermas. For a detailed treatment, see *Ibid.* 43-77.
[61] With the exception of the last fact, which is still granted by most critical scholars.

C. Fact #1: Jesus' _____ on the

_____

My Drawing:

7. You can remember this fact by remembering the word
   "_____."

8. We already know that four, separate, ancient documents report this fact: The New Testament gospels.

9. But did you know Jesus' death by crucifixion is also mentioned by five, ancient, non-Christian sources?

a. _____

    i. A Jewish historian

    ii. "When Pilate, upon hearing him accused by men of the highest standing amongst us, had condemned him to be crucified..." [62]

b. _____

    i. A Roman historian

    ii. "Nero fastened the guilt (of the burning of Rome) and inflicted the most exquisite tortures on a class hated for their abominations, called Christians by the populace. Christus, from whom the name had its origin, suffered the extreme penalty during the reign of Tiberius at the hands of one of our procurators, Pontius Pilate." [63]

c. _____**of Samosata**

    i. A Greek author

    ii. "The Christians, you know, worship a man to this day—the distinguished personage who introduced their novel rites, and was crucified on that account." [64]

---

[62] *Antiquities of the Jews* 18.3.3 (#64). Quoted in *Jesus Under Fire: Modern Scholarship Reinvents the Historical Jesus*, ed. Michael J. Wilkins and J. P. Moreland (Grand Rapids, MI: Zondervan, 1996), 212.

[63] *The Annals* 15.44. Quoted in *The Case for the Resurrection of Jesus*, 49.

[64] Lucian of Samosata, *The Death of Peregrine* 11-13. Quoted in ibid.

d. _____ **Bar-Serapion**
   i.   A prisoner who wrote a letter to his son
   ii. "What advantage came to the Jews by the murder of their Wise King, seeing that from that very time their kingdom was driven away from them?" [65]

e. _____
   i.   A Jewish Rabbinical text[66]
   ii. "On the eve of the Passover, Yeshu was hanged."

D. Fact #2: The disciples'_____ that they saw Jesus after he _____ from the dead.

My Drawing

---

[65] Quoted in ibid.

[66] Babylonian Talmud, *Sanhedrin* 43a. Quoted in ibid. *Yeshu* is Joshua in Hebrew, the equivalent is *Iesous* in Greek or Jesus in English. Being hung on a tree was a way Jews would talk about crucifixion at that time (Luke 23:39 and Galatians 3:13).

4. You can remember this fact by remembering the word
   "_____"

5. We know they claimed it

   a. You can remember the evidence for this by remembering
      the word, "POW!"

   b. _____ **testimony** about the apostles
      i.   Paul knew them personally and he said they were
           claiming Jesus rose.
      ii. 1 Cor. 15:3-11

   c. _____ **Tradition** of the early church

      i.   **Creeds:** These are just like the lyrics to a song that
           you can't get out of your head. They're a way to
           preserve and memorize important information.

           a)   1 Cor. 15:3-5

           b)   This creed says Jesus appeared to his disciples
                and others.

ii.   **Sermon Summaries:** These are the *Cliff's Notes* of the apostles' earliest teachings in the book of Acts.

d.   _____ **documents**

i.   The Gospels

ii.   Apostolic Fathers

2. Not only did they claim it, they really believed it!

    a. They were _____ to the point

       where they willing to suffer and _____ for saying

       Jesus rose from the dead and appeared to them.

    b. _____ ancient sources document their willingness to die for their claim

       i. Acts
       ii. Clement of Rome[67]
       iii. Polycarp
       iv. Ignatius[68]
       v. Dionysius of Corinth
       vi. Tertullian[69]
       vii. Origen[70]

---

[67] He documented Peter and Paul's sufferings and execution for their claims.

[68] He wrote, "when Jesus came to those with Peter, he said to them: 'take, handle me and see that I am not a bodiless demon' and immediately they handled him and believed, having known his flesh and blood. Because of this they despised death; but beyond death they were found." Quoted in *Ibid.* 57

[69] He reports Paul was beheaded and Peter was crucified by Nero. He adds that anyone could check it out in "The Lives of the Caesars" because these things are matters of public record. *Ibid.* 58

[70] He reports that Peter was crucified upside down and Paul was beheaded by Nero. *Ibid.*

3. The apostles' died for their own testimony that they had

_____ seen Jesus alive after his crucifixion.

E. Fact #3: The conversion of the

_____, _____.

My Drawing

1. You can remember fact #3 and #4 by remembering two
   letters: _____ & _____

2. Paul _____ became a Christian

   a. _____ Report: Within three years of the time
      he became a Christian, there was a story going around
      about him in Judea (Gal. 1:2-23).

b. _____ **Report:** Luke wrote about how Paul (aka Saul of Tarsus) persecuted the church and was even involved in the murder of the first Christian martyr, Stephen.

c. _____ **Report:** Paul's own words about why he became a Christian are documented in letters he wrote to churches in Corinth, Galatia, & Philppi.

3. Paul _____ and _____ for his belief
   a. He died for his belief, just like the original disciples did.
   b. The evidence for his suffering and death includes documents written by himself, Luke, Clement of Rome, Polycarp, Tertullian, Dionysius of Corinth, and Origen.

F. Fact #4: The conversion of the

_____, _____.

1. Jesus' brothers and sisters
   a. The Gospels report that Jesus had at least four brothers (Matt. 13:55-56; Mark 6:3).

    b. The Jewish historian, Josephus, mentions "the brother of Jesus, who was called Christ, whose name was James."[71]

2. James _____ a Christian

    i. **Before** (Mark 3:21, 31; 6:3-4; John 7:5)

    ii. **Creed** (1 Cor. 15:3-7)

    iii. **After** (Acts 15:12-21; Gal. 1:19)

3. James _____for his belief

    i. Not only did James become a Christian and lead the Jerusalem church, but he died for his claim.

---

[71] Josephus, *Antiquities of the Jews* 20.9.1 (#200). *Christian Classics Ethereal Library*, http://www.ccel.org/j/josephus/works/ant-20.htm (accessed November 25, 2010).

ii. The fact that James dies for his belief is documented by non-Christian and Christian sources.[72]

    i. Josephus

    ii. Hegesippus

    iii. Clement of Alexandria

G. Fact #5: The _____ _____ [73]

My Drawing

---

[72] Neither Hegesippus' work or Clement's mention of this in the *Hypotyposes* have survived since the 2nd century. However, records of their reports survive in quotations by Eusebius.

[73] Facts #1-4 are granted by nearly every critical scholar who studies this subject. Fact #5 is granted only by a majority of critical scholars (about 75%).

1. You can remember this fact by remembering the word
   "_____."

2. _____ Factor

3. _____ didn't deny it

4. _____ of Women

5. **Here's the point of all this:** If the tomb was empty because Jesus really rose from the dead, then God exists, Christianity is true, and eternal life is possible and available to you.

Works Cited

Habermas, Gary R., and Michael Licona. *The Case for the Resurrection of Jesus.* Grand Rapids, MI: Kregel Publications, 2004.

Jesus Under Fire: Modern Scholarship Reinvents the Historical Jesus. Edited by Michael J. Wilkins and J. P. Moreland. Grand Rapids, MI: Zondervan, 1996.

Josephus. "Antiquities of the Jews - Book Xx." *Christian Classics Ethereal Library.* http://www.ccel.org/j/josephus/works/ant-20.htm (accessed November 25, 2010).

Workbook Answers

Looking for the answers to the fill-in-the-blanks? You've come to the right place. Putting answers in the back of the book is a long-standing academic tradition, probably dating back to your 3rd grade math class! ☺

Download the complete notes for each lesson in this workbook at:
http://www.ApologeticsGuy.com/answers

Use this code: Confidence123109

Get More Accessible Apologetics Training

Access Mikel's articles, curriculum, online classes, audio lectures and other helpful resources at **ApologeticsGuy.com**—the street-level apologetics blog for everyday defenders of the faith.

Made in the USA
Lexington, KY
14 July 2012